The Little Book of Edible Insects

Discover, Cook, and Taste the Foods of Tomorrow

By

Timéo Grimes

Table of contents :

INTRODUCTION

For millennia, insects have shared our planet, seamlessly integrating into our ecosystems, yet they have seldom found a place at our table. What is now considered exotic or futuristic food is, in reality, an ancient tradition in many cultures around the world.

This little book invites you to delve into the fascinating world of edible insects—six-legged creatures challenging culinary norms long-established. Beyond the initial surprise, you will discover that these tiny beings offer more than just an eccentric plate appearance: they signify a path towards more sustainable eating, a source of valuable protein for our planet, and a palette of flavors and textures to explore.

Hunting, farming, cooking, and tasting insects are not acts of marginal curiosity but steps toward a gastronomic revolution slowly but surely taking shape. Insects are the foods of tomorrow, and it's time to incorporate them into our daily lives.

Throughout the pages of this book, we will explore the history of insect consumption, their nutritional benefits, various methods of preparation, traditional and modern recipes, and the promising future they paint for a more planet-friendly diet.

Whether you're a fearless culinary adventurer, an environmental advocate, or simply curious by nature, this book is an invitation to immerse yourself in a new taste dimension and rethink our relationship with food. It's time to discover, cook, and taste the foods of tomorrow. Are you ready to venture into the world of edible insects?

Chapter 1: Edible Insects Throughout History

The History of Insect Consumption Across Civilizations

The practice of consuming insects dates back thousands of years, spanning millennia and influencing various civilizations globally. In many ancient societies, insects were not just a food source but an integral element of their culture and way of life.

In tropical regions of Asia, Africa, and South America, indigenous peoples long recognized the nutritional richness of insects, regularly incorporating bees, ants, grasshoppers, silkworms, and more into their diets. These insects were not only consumed for their nutritional value but also used in traditional medicine and ritual ceremonies.

In Asia, crickets and silkworms were domesticated over 2,000 years ago, marking the beginning of large-scale insect farming. The Mayans in Central America prepared dishes with grasshoppers long before the arrival of Spanish conquistadors. In Africa, termites were and still are considered an essential protein source.

Evolution of Perceptions of Insects as a Food Source

Despite their rich culinary heritage, insects underwent a complex evolution in how they were perceived as a food source. With the rise of agriculture and urbanization, many societies gradually shifted away from insect consumption in favor of other animal protein sources like livestock.

This transition was influenced by factors such as cultural and religious norms, changing taste preferences, and constraints related to food access. For instance, in Jewish and Muslim traditions, certain insects are considered non-kosher or haram, contributing to these communities distancing themselves from insect consumption.

However, the modern era has witnessed a renewed interest in insects as food. Scientists, aware of their nutritional value and low environmental impact, began promoting insect consumption as a sustainable solution to global food challenges. This reevaluation of insects as a food source was reinforced by movements like entomophagy, encouraging deliberate insect consumption for ecological and nutritional reasons.

Cultural and Ecological Reasons for Insect Consumption

Insect consumption has always been influenced by cultural and ecological factors. In many parts of the world, insects were and still are considered delicious delicacies, offering unique flavors and textures to traditional dishes.

From an ecological perspective, insects offer a considerable advantage over other animal protein sources. They require fewer resources in terms of food and water, produce fewer greenhouse gases, and occupy less space than livestock. This reduced environmental footprint makes them a crucial option to address the challenges of food sustainability in the era of global population growth and climate change.

This chapter, therefore, explores the rich and intricate history of insect consumption across civilizations, shedding light on the evolving perception of these small creatures as a food source while highlighting the cultural and ecological motivations underlying their consumption. It's a journey through time and space to understand how insects have been and continue to be an essential part of the human food landscape.

Chapter 2: Biodiversity of Edible Insects

Exploring Edible Insect Species Worldwide

The biodiversity of edible insects is truly remarkable, encompassing a multitude of species with varied forms, sizes, and flavors. As entomophagy, or insect consumption, gains popularity, it's crucial to recognize that this practice is not limited to a handful of species. In fact, thousands of different insects are consumed worldwide, each contributing to local gastronomy in its unique way.

From crispy crickets in Mexico to palm weevil larvae in Southeast Asia and fried grasshoppers in sub-Saharan Africa, each region develops its preferences for edible insects. Some are valued for their nutty taste, while others for their slightly acidic flavor or crunchy texture. This chapter takes you on a sensory journey through the most commonly consumed insect species worldwide, revealing the richness and diversity of this overlooked food source.

Different Categories of Insects (Terrestrial, Aquatic, etc.)

The biodiversity of edible insects is not limited to species alone but extends to the various habitats these creatures inhabit. Insects can be found in a multitude of environments, from fields and forests to rivers and lakes. This diversity of habitats results in a variety of terrestrial, aquatic, and semi-aquatic insects available for consumption.

Terrestrial insects like crickets and grasshoppers are commonly consumed in many parts of the world, with their muscular legs and jumping ability making them abundant protein sources. Aquatic insects include species like aquatic insect larvae, dragonflies, and even sea worms. Their availability depends on the proximity to fresh or saltwater, and they are often prepared differently based on their habitat.

Environmental Benefits of the Diversity of Edible Insects

Beyond their intrinsic variety, the diversity of edible insects has notable environmental advantages. Compared to more conventional animal protein production methods, insect farming and harvesting require fewer resources in terms of food and water. They also emit fewer greenhouse gases and occupy less space. This reduced environmental footprint makes them a crucial option to address the challenges of food sustainability in the era of global population growth and climate change.

Chapter 3: Nutritional Benefits of Insects

Nutritional Composition of Insects (Proteins, Lipids, Vitamins, etc.)

Edible insects are nutritional powerhouses, offering an exceptional nutritional composition. They are particularly rich in high-quality proteins, often providing as much or more protein than many traditional meats. For instance, crickets consist of approximately 60 to 70% protein, while silkworms are known for their high essential amino acid content.

Insects are also a significant source of lipids, with a substantial portion being composed of beneficial unsaturated fatty acids. Moreover, they are packed with essential vitamins such as B12, D, various B vitamins, and minerals like iron and zinc.

Comparison with Other Animal and Plant Protein Sources

When comparing insects to other animal and plant protein sources, it becomes evident that they have a considerably lower environmental impact. Insect farming requires less water, space, and food per unit of protein produced compared to livestock, for example. Additionally, greenhouse gas production is significantly reduced.

In terms of proteins, insects can compete with traditional animal sources such as beef, chicken, and fish, while having a clear nutritional advantage in terms of amino acid composition and healthy fat content.

Compared to plant proteins, insects offer a more comprehensive nutritional profile, making them a nutrient-rich alternative. They often contain higher levels of vitamins and minerals, making them particularly appealing for those looking to diversify their plant-based diet.

Health Benefits of Insect Consumption

Insect consumption also provides health benefits. Their nutritionally rich profile, including proteins, unsaturated fatty acids, vitamins, and minerals, makes them a healthy food source. Unsaturated fatty acids, for example, are associated with better heart health.

Moreover, some insects contain bioactive compounds such as antioxidants, which may contribute to the prevention of various diseases. The health benefits of insect consumption are still widely studied, but early research suggests they could play a role in reducing the risks of chronic diseases.

This chapter delves into the nutritional composition of insects, comparisons with other protein sources, and the health benefits associated with their consumption, providing a comprehensive understanding of why these small creatures are increasingly considered a valuable and sustainable food source.

Chapter 4: Hunting, Rearing, and Harvesting Insects

Methods for Hunting Insects in the Wild

Hunting insects in the wild is an ancient and diverse practice that varies based on regions and targeted species. It often requires in-depth knowledge of insect ecology and behavior, along with specific collection skills. Hunting methods include the use of nets, traps, ultraviolet lamps, and even more traditional techniques such as manual harvesting.

In many cultures, insect hunting is a seasonal activity involving specific techniques based on the time of year and insect habits. For example, migratory locusts can be captured during their massive movements, while insect larvae can be found under tree bark or in the soil.

Home or Business Insect Farming

Insect farming is an increasingly common method to ensure a consistent supply of edible insects. This practice allows precise control over the environment, nutrition, and growth of insects. Insects raised are often intended for human consumption but can also be used for animal feed or even industrial applications, such as insect flour production.

Commonly farmed insects include crickets, mealworms, grasshoppers, and beetle larvae. Insect farming can be carried out on a small scale at home, in micro-farm facilities, or on a larger scale in specialized farms. It requires careful attention to the living conditions of insects, their diet, and growth.

Harvesting, Sorting, and Preparing Edible Insects

Insect harvesting is a crucial step that requires specific skills to avoid damaging specimens and ensure their quality. Once harvested, insects need to be sorted to remove impurities such as plant debris or other small organisms. Subsequently, they are prepared for consumption, which may include cleaning, cooking, drying, or seasoning.

The preparation of edible insects varies considerably based on culinary traditions and regional preferences. Some prefer them fried and crispy, while others incorporate them into more elaborate dishes. Insect-based recipes have multiplied in recent years, becoming a source of inspiration for chefs and culinary enthusiasts worldwide.

This chapter details methods for hunting insects, home or business farming, as well as the steps for harvesting, sorting, and preparing edible insects. It offers a practical overview of different approaches to integrate these small creatures into our diet.

Chapter 5: Cooking and Recipes with Insects

Tips for Deliciously Preparing and Cooking Insects

Cooking with insects requires a creative and respectful approach to make the most of these unique ingredients. Here are some practical tips for preparing and cooking insects to bring out their delicious flavors and textures.

Start with thorough insect preparation, ensuring they are cleaned meticulously to eliminate any traces of dirt. Cooking is also crucial; insects can be fried, grilled, roasted, or steamed, depending on the desired texture. Experimenting with different cooking methods is recommended to highlight the characteristics of each species.

Regarding seasoning, the possibilities are endless. Insects pair well with a variety of spices, herbs, and sauces. Using familiar or exotic seasonings can create balanced and flavorful dishes.

Traditional Recipes from Different Regions of the World

Edible insects have long been an integral part of traditional cuisine in many regions worldwide. Let's explore some traditional insect-based recipes that reflect the diversity of culinary practices globally.

In Mexico, chapulines, spiced fried grasshoppers, are a popular snack. In Malaysia, sago worms, butterfly larvae sautéed in palm oil, are enthusiastically enjoyed. In Thailand, fried silkworm pupae, pupae of silkworms fried to perfection, are a cherished delicacy. Each of these recipes reflects the ingenuity and creativity of local cuisines in leveraging available natural resources.

Creating Modern Dishes with Insects

Cooking with insects extends beyond traditional recipes; it provides fertile ground for gastronomic innovation. Contemporary chefs turn to insects to add a touch of originality to their creations. Discover how insects are used as ingredients in sophisticated dishes, original appetizers, bold pastries, and even elaborate cocktails. Integrating insects into modern cuisine offers a palette of unique flavors and an opportunity to push the boundaries of culinary creativity.

This chapter guides you through the art of cooking with insects, offering practical tips, traditional recipes from around the world, and inspiring ideas to explore new taste dimensions.

Chapter 6: Edible Insects in Contemporary Cuisine

The Growing Influence of Edible Insects in Gastronomy

Edible insects are rapidly gaining popularity, exerting a growing influence on the world of gastronomy. Today, more chefs and restaurants are turning to insects to enrich their menus. This trend reflects a shift towards more sustainable and creative cooking.

Recognition of the nutritional qualities of insects and their low environmental impact has prompted many chefs to incorporate them into their culinary creations. They see insects as versatile ingredients capable of bringing unique flavors and an ecological dimension to their dishes.

Restaurants and Chefs Embracing Insects in Their Menus

Numerous culinary establishments worldwide have embraced the edible insect revolution. From Michelin-starred restaurants to local bistros, many talented chefs showcase insects in their culinary creations.

These chefs stand out for their creativity and boldness. They develop sophisticated dishes featuring insects, from appetizers to desserts. Some establishments even specialize exclusively in insect-based cuisine, offering diners a unique and immersive culinary experience.

Upcoming Culinary Trends Related to Insects

The edible insect trend in contemporary cuisine shows no signs of slowing down. On the contrary, it continues to evolve and diversify. Insects are increasingly used in processed food products, such as energy bars, pasta, and snacks.

Upcoming trends could include a greater integration of insects into vegan and vegetarian cuisine, providing an alternative source of animal protein. Additionally, culinary research is exploring new methods of preparing and presenting insects to make them even more appealing to consumers.

In conclusion, edible insects have secured a prominent place in contemporary cuisine, stimulating innovation and creativity among chefs worldwide. Their growing influence on gastronomy is a fascinating trend to follow, promising to shape the future of our diet in a sustainable and delicious manner.

Chapter 7: The Future of Edible Insects

Challenges and Opportunities in the Edible Insect Industry

The edible insect industry is experiencing rapid growth, but it faces significant challenges. One of the main obstacles is varying regulations from country to country, which can hinder the development of this new food source. Edible insect producers are closely collaborating with regulatory bodies to establish food safety standards and ensure product quality.

However, this industry also presents enormous opportunities. Insects are a sustainable and resource-efficient protein source. Startups and agri-food companies are investing in research and development to create innovative insect-based products, ranging from meat substitutes to pet foods. The industry has the potential to become a new backbone of the global food supply.

Technological Innovations and New Insect-Based Food Sources

Technological innovations play a key role in the development of the edible insect industry. New farming and harvesting techniques are being developed to make production more efficient and sustainable. Companies are also exploring methods to process insects into flours, oils, and versatile food ingredients.

New insect-based food sources are also emerging. Researchers are working on applications such as 3D printing of insect-based foods, offering endless possibilities for creating customized and nutritious food products.

Prospects for More Sustainable Food with Insects

The future of edible insects aligns with a broader vision of more sustainable food. Insects are a response to the challenges of food security, resource consumption, and climate change. Their low environmental footprint, exceptional nutritional profile, and versatility make them a promising option to feed a growing global population.

The use of insects in both human and animal food can contribute to reducing deforestation, greenhouse gas emissions, and pressure on natural resources. They also provide an opportunity for farmers to diversify their income and contribute to more sustainable agriculture.

In conclusion, the future of edible insects is promising but requires ongoing collaboration among researchers, industry, regulators, and consumers. Together, we can harness the potential of insects to create a more sustainable, nutritious, and environmentally friendly food future.

CONCLUSION

The world of edible insects is constantly evolving, offering a fascinating glimpse into the future of our food. This brief book has explored various aspects of this culinary revolution, from the history of insect consumption through the ages to contemporary trends and technological innovations. It has also highlighted the challenges facing this rapidly growing industry and the opportunities it presents for more sustainable food.

As we look to the future, it's clear that edible insects have a crucial role to play in realizing our vision of environmentally friendly food. Their low ecological footprint, exceptional nutritional composition, and versatility position them at the forefront of the transition to sustainable eating.

However, for this transition to succeed, it is crucial for all stakeholders, from producers to consumers, regulators to researchers, to work in harmony. Food safety standards must be established and adhered to, research and development encouraged, and public education on the benefits of edible insects pursued.

Ultimately, edible insects are not just an alternative protein source but also a symbol of our ability to innovate and adapt to future food challenges. By incorporating them into our diet, we can contribute to a more sustainable future where food is both delicious, nutritious, and planet-friendly. So, let your culinary adventure with insects begin, as the future of food is promising and buzzing with opportunities.